The Modern Juicer

To my girls, Miranda and Alba. To my family and friends, with all my heart.
To Jaco, for his tireless help, with all my love.

We would like to thank Dr. Ramon Roselló for allowing the reproduction
of several of his recipes.

The Modern Juicer

52 Dairy-Free Drink Recipes Using Rice, Oats, Barley, Soy, and Vegetables

María del Mar Gómez

Skyhorse Publishing

CONTENTS

INTRODUCTION

Why Choose Vegetable Drinks?

Milk is and has been one of mankind's most basic foods for hundreds of years. Not only milk, but also other dairy products produced from it, like yogurt, cream, and cheese. This is because milk contains a great variety of nutrients that are beneficial for our bodies.

But is it really necessary to consume milk to feed our bodies and minds? In terms of nutrients, the answer is yes. For instance, it has minerals (phosphorus, zinc, and magnesium), proteins (casein, lactalbumins, and lactoglobulins), vitamins (especially vitamin B), and carbohydrates (lactose). Milk also contains calcium, which is essential for strong and healthy bones.

For a long time, milk has been considered to be one of the healthiest foods for our bodies. Only in recent times has it become clear that it has several side effects that we can't ignore, and this realization not only sheds a new light on its nutritional value but makes the case that milk may not be recommended for consumption by adults.

Many of the presumed benefits of milk are actually now considered to be detrimental to our overall health. For example, it is important to talk about calcium because, in Western medicine, calcium content is presented as the main reason *for* consuming milk. It's true that milk is rich in calcium, but, as a matter of fact, when we consume milk, most of this calcium transforms into calcium phosphate and is expelled from the body in the feces. Therefore, we can't use it. Other foods give us more calcium, like legumes, nuts, and vegetables. Their calcium content is not as rich, but it is better assimilated into the body.

On the other hand, there are many people that show symptoms of lactose intolerance. And, even though the data is not yet conclusive, it is believed that half of the world's population may suffer from this condition, lactose being the main carbohydrate contained

ADVANTAGES OF A MILK-FREE DIET IN ADULTS

Did you know that humans are the only animals that consume the milk of another species once the breastfeeding period is over? There are countless studies that prove that removing milk from ones diet is not a risk for bones, as long as one follows a sensible diet. For instance, Harvard University conducted a twelve year study on seventy-eight thousand women and found that not drinking milk, or drinking only small quantities, did not increase the risk of osteoporosis. Another, more curious example: Despite not drinking animal milk, African Bantu women don't suffer from bone problems associated with lack of calcium. It's also important to keep in mind that each Bantu woman has, on average, eight children whom she must breastfeed herself.

in milk. This intolerance is a consequence of the lack of an enzyme, lactase, which metabolizes lactose. Common symptoms are diarrhea, gas, abdominal pain, and weight loss.

If you are lactose intolerant, your doctor will surely advise you to eliminate all dairy from your diet. As you may know, you can get the required calcium from other sources, such as various vegetable.

Let's continue discussing the negative properties of milk. Another disadvantage is its high content of saturated fats. Although this depends on the type of milk and its processing method, whole milk can be up to seventy percent saturated fats (the unhealthy type) and thirty percent unsaturated fats (the healthy kind that regulates cholesterol). The problem, besides the high amount of saturated fats, is that pasteurization and homogenization weaken the unsaturated fats, which thereby weakens the unsaturated fat's ability to fight cholesterol.

The intent here is not to be alarming, but it's clear that there isn't the need to consume milk to enjoy a healthy and nourishing diet. Milk includes more than seventy different hormones (cattle are given growth hormones and many others) and countless other toxins caused by the industrialization of our society, which are not safe for our bodies.

This book gives you an alternative to milk in the form of vegetable drinks, which are much healthier for the body. It is not necessary to eliminate milk forever if you do not want to. But if you do remove it from your diet, it certainly won't harm you at all because you can get all the calcium you need from other foods, as previously mentioned. Simply put, this introduction serves to give you the necessary information for you to decide whether the consumption of milk is appropriate for you.

The following recipes will show you how you can make dairy-free vegetable drinks with a large selection of ingredients: hazelnuts, almonds, millet, coconut, rice, etc. This will provide you with enough variety of milk substitutes to suit any taste. Furthermore, they are very easy to prepare.

We hope this book proves to be a welcome discovery, one that exposes you to the varied and delicious world of vegetable drinks that will introduce new flavors into your diet while helping you improve your health.

BASIC RECIPE

Making and Straining Vegetable Drinks

Most of the vegetable drinks in this book are made in a similar fashion. Whether using a blender, juicer, or food processor, you need to blend water with the other ingredients. For some recipes it is necessary to soak the hazelnuts or to add other ingredients after processing the mixture.

On the other hand, during the preparation of vegetable drinks, it's very important to strain the mixture to avoid lumps or any other residue so that the resulting drink is smooth and tasty. All recipes require straining the mixture, and we recommend that you follow these steps:

1. The utensils you need for straining are a cheese cloth, a large bowl, a colander, and a large spoon.
2. When the mixture is ready, put the colander over the bowl and cover it with the cheesecloth. Pour the mixture into the colander.
3. The mixture will seep into the bowl.
4. Use a large spoon to press the solids and help them to release the remaining liquid.

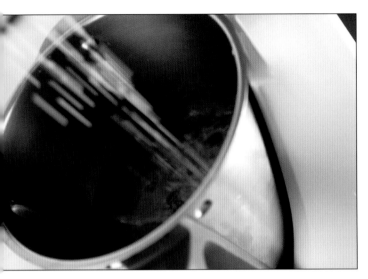

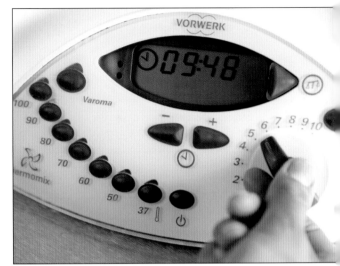

WITH OR WITHOUT SUGAR?

Sugar and other sweeteners are some of the ingredients that are always used in the recipes of this book. You may decide not to use them, but a lot of people might then feel these drinks are boring and flavorless. However, in the ingredients list of each recipe, I suggest the necessary amount of sugar to give a sweet note to any vegetable drink. While you will decide to use white or brown sugar, dark brown sugar is recommended because it is not as highly processed.

Industrialized sugars (obtained by processing sugar cane, beets, etc.) are very high in calories, are addictive, and cause cavities in the teeth. According to M. O. Bruker, a German MD, sugar is a "calcium thief," which means that it weakens bones. Sugar also increases the risk of developing stomach ulcers, liver problems, and atherosclerosis.

There is a great variety of sweeteners, like fructose, aspartame, and others, that have been used as sugar substitutes. They also are not good for the body; for example, aspartame (two hundred times more sweet than sugar) causes the accumulation of phenylalanine and methanol in the body.

In any case, if you choose to use artificial sweeteners, add them to the vegetable drink towards the end of the process because they are affected by the heat produced by the blender. Afterwards, you will have to stir to ensure the drink is evenly and properly sweetened.

Another popular option is fructose, but to get a small amount of this it is necessary to process many pounds of fruits, wasting a significant amount of fruit to produce a tiny amount of fructose.

I recommend brown sugar or honey to sweeten your vegetable drinks. Use enough sugar to suit your taste, but if you are going to use these drinks in a savory dish, skip this step and don't add sugar.

RICE DRINKS

Benefits of Rice Drinks

A rice-based drink is certainly one of the most appealing vegetable drinks. It has a nice and subtle flavor and is easily digested—highly recommended if you have digestive issues, like gastritis, ulcers, or slow digestion. A glass of a cold rice drink can even help a pregnant woman overcome nausea.

Athletes, children, and teenagers alike benefit from the carbohydrates contained in rice. These are slow-release carbohydrates that provide constant energy to the body without varying glucose levels in the blood (this happens if we consume refined sugar). So, as long as you don't add sugar to the recipe, this is a great drink for diabetics.

This high energy quality does not go hand in hand with more calories. For instance, rice has about half the calories of almonds and soy, so if you are trying to lose some pounds, rice drinks should be a part of your diet.

Another reason for consuming rice drinks is that they lower high blood pressure, thanks to its low sodium and its high potassium content. It does not have much protein (although it is high quality), but it is rich in magnesium, a fundamental mineral for healthy bones and oxygen transportation, and for its concentration of polyunsaturated fatty acids, which regulate cholesterol and triglycerides levels. Rice drinks also help eliminate uric acid, making it very helpful for people suffering from gout. And for those seeking a delicious drink, you can now find rice drinks with almonds or hazelnuts in stores.

Finally, keep in mind that brown rice is always more nutritious than white rice. Shake the drink well before serving, especially if it has been sitting in the refrigerator for a while. It is also worthwhile to soak rice for at least four hours before processing because not all blenders or food processors are equally powerful. This will make blending easier.

DELICIOUS FOR HEALTHY PEOPLE . . . AND IDEAL FOR THE ILL

Besides being very tasty, rice drinks are a high energy food, are easy to digest, and are gluten free—suitable for any kind of diet.

Basic Rice Drink Recipe

Ingredients

    6 cups water
    2 tablespoons (30 gr) Thai or Basmati rice
    1 tablespoon sesame oil
    4 tablespoons (60 gr) sugar
    1 teaspoon vanilla sugar or vanilla extract
    Pinch of sea salt

Preparation

1. Put all the ingredients in the blender and process until smooth.
2. Strain as instructed in the basic recipe (page 12).

Coarse Rice Drink

Ingredients

    6 cups water
    2 tablespoons (30 gr) white rice
    1 teaspoon sunflower oil
    4 tablespoons (60 gr) sugar
    1 teaspoon vanilla sugar or vanilla extract
    Pinch of sea salt

Preparation

1. Put the ingredients in the blender and process until smooth.
2. Strain as instructed in the basic recipe (page 12).

Calcium-Rich Rice Drink

Ingredients

  6 cups water
  2 ½ tablespoons (30 gr) Thai or Basmati rice
  ⅔ cup (100 gr) sesame seeds
  1 tablespoon sesame oil
  5 tablespoons + 2 teaspoons (70 gr) sugar
  1 teaspoon vanilla sugar or vanilla extract
  Pinch of sea salt

Preparation
1. Put the ingredients in the blender and process until smooth.
2. Strain as instructed in the basic recipe (page 12).

Rice Drink with Cinnamon

Ingredients

 6 cups water
 2 ½ tablespoons (30 gr) Thai or Basmati rice
 1 teaspoon ground cinnamon
 3 drops cinnamon extract
 1 tablespoon sesame oil
 4 tablespoons (60 gr) sugar
 1 teaspoon vanilla sugar or vanilla extract
 Pinch of sea salt

Preparation

1. Put the ingredients in the blender and process until smooth.
2. Strain as instructed in the basic recipe (page 12).

Rice Drink with Wild Fruits

Ingredients

    6 cups water
    2 ½ tablespoons (30 gr) Thai or Basmati rice
    4 ounces (100 gr) wild fruits
    1 tablespoon sesame oil
    8 tablespoons (120 gr) sugar
    1 teaspoon vanilla sugar or vanilla extract
    Pinch of sea salt

Preparation

1. Put the ingredients in the blender and process until smooth.
2. Strain as instructed in the basic recipe (page 12).

Rice Drink with Dehydrated Fruits

Ingredients
 6 cups water
 2 ½ tablespoons (30 gr) Thai or Basmati rice
 ⅔ cup (60 gr) dehydrated fruits (banana, papaya, pineapple, apple, etc.)
 1 tablespoon sesame oil
 4 tablespoons (60 gr) sugar
 1 teaspoon vanilla sugar or vanilla extract
 Pinch of sea salt

Preparation
1. Put the ingredients in the blender and process until smooth.
2. Strain as instructed in the basic recipe (page 12).

Rice Drink with Dried Fruits

Ingredients

    6 cups water
    2 ½ tablespoons (30 gr) Thai or Basmati rice
    ½ cup (60 gr) dried fruits (dates, prunes, raisins, apples, figs, etc.)
    1 tablespoon sesame oil
    7 tablespoons + 1 teaspoon (80 gr) sugar
    1 teaspoon vanilla sugar or vanilla extract
    Pinch of sea salt

Preparation

1. Put the ingredients in the blender and process until smooth.
2. Strain as instructed in the basic recipe (page 12).

Rice Drink with Nuts

Ingredients
- 6 cups water
- 2 ½ tablespoons (30 gr) Thai or Basmati rice
- ⅔ cup (90 gr) nuts (hazelnuts, almonds, macadamias, peanuts, etc.)
- 1 tablespoon sesame oil
- 7 tablespoons (100 gr) sugar
- 1 teaspoon vanilla sugar or vanilla extract
- Pinch of sea salt

Preparation
1. Put the ingredients in the blender and process until smooth.
2. Strain as instructed in the basic recipe (page 12).

Brown Basmati Rice Drink

Ingredients

    6 cups water
    2 ½ tablespoons (30 gr) Thai or Basmati rice
    1 tablespoon sunflower oil
    4 tablespoons + 2 teaspoons (70 gr) sugar
    1 teaspoon vanilla sugar or vanilla extract
    Pinch of sea salt

Preparation

1. Put the ingredients in the blender and process until smooth.
2. Strain as instructed in the basic recipe (page 12).

Paradise Rice Drink

Ingredients
    6 cups water
    2 ½ tablespoons (30 gr) Thai or Basmati rice
    1 tablespoon sesame oil
    1 teaspoon vanilla sugar or vanilla extract
    7 tablespoons + 1 teaspoon (80 gr) sugar
    Pinch of sea salt

Infusion
    1¼ cup (300 ml) water
    1 teaspoon thyme
    1 teaspoon eucalyptus
    1 teaspoon rosemary
    1 teaspoon mint

Preparation
1. **For the infusion:** Boil the water and add the herbs. Let steep for five minutes before straining.
2. Put the ingredients and the infusion in the blender. Process until smooth.
3. Strain as instructed in the basic recipe (page 12).

Coarse Brown Rice Drink

Ingredients
    6 cups water
    2 ½ tablespoons (30 gr) brown rice
    1 tablespoon sunflower oil
    5 tablespoons + 2 teaspoons (70 grs) sugar
    1 teaspoon vanilla sugar or vanilla extract
    Pinch of sea salt

Preparation
1. Put the ingredients in the blender and process until smooth.
2. Strain as instructed in the basic recipe (page 12).

Rice Drink with Mint

Ingredients

    6 cups water
    2 ½ tablespoons (30 gr) Thai or Basmati rice
    3 fresh mint leaves
    1 tablespoon sesame oil
    6 tablespoons (90 gr) sugar
    1 teaspoon vanilla sugar or vanilla extract
    Pinch of sea salt

Preparation

1. Put the ingredients in the blender and process until smooth.
2. Strain as instructed in the basic recipe (page 12).

Rice Drink with Lemon

Ingredients

    6 cups water
    2 ½ tablespoons (30 gr) Thai or Basmati rice
    The peel of one lemon
    1 tablespoon sesame oil
    7 tablespoons (100 gr) sugar
    1 teaspoon vanilla sugar or vanilla extract
    Pinch of sea salt

Preparation

1. Put the ingredients in the blender and process until smooth.
2. Strain as instructed in the basic recipe (page 12).

Rice Drink with Orange

Ingredients

  6 cups water
  2 ½ tablespoons (30 gr) Thai or Basmati rice
  The peel of one orange
  1 tablespoon sesame oil
  7 tablespoons (100 gr) sugar
  1 teaspoon vanilla sugar or vanilla extract
  Pinch of sea salt

Preparation

1. Put the ingredients in the blender and process until smooth.
2. Strain as instructed in the basic recipe (page 12).

OAT DRINKS

Benefits of Oat Drinks

Oat drinks are a favorite of children because they are very flavorful, despite not having any sugar. However, you may add sugar or honey, if you prefer. But why don't you try it without any sweeteners, just for a day? Another option is to add a half teaspoon of ground cinnamon for an unusual and somewhat sweet flavor.

Oatmeal is a nourishing cereal, rich in proteins and unsaturated fats and excellent for your health. Besides, it has a good amount of B vitamins, essential for the nervous system. These vitamins, plus the alkaloid avenin, has a soothing effect on the nervous system. So, consuming oats on a regular basis can give you a degree of tranquility.

Just like rice drinks, oat drinks are good for active people that need a lot of energy (for example, to deal with the stress of daily life or for athletic activities) because it provides generous amounts of slow-release carbohydrates. Make it a part of your diet, especially when you are under very intense mental or physical activities.

On the other hand, oatmeal is a welcome snack, calming hunger pangs without many calories thanks to its high starch content that transforms itself into maltodextrin, glucose, and maltose. In this way, the body receives low-absorption sugars that stimulate the thyroid gland and cause a feeling of satiety.

It is advisable to soak oatmeal for at least four hours before processing in the blender.

OAT DRINKS: HIGH IN FIBER

Oat drinks are some of the richest in fiber of all the vegetable drinks. As you might know, fiber is not only important for the regulation of bowel movements, but it also plays an indispensable role in the proper function of the cardiovascular system. It also helps recover the intestinal flora (essential to keep the digestive process in good shape) thanks to its beta-glucans, which are essential for the body. If you suffer from fluid retention or constipation, oat drinks are highly recommended.

Basic Oat Drink Recipe

Ingredients

    6 cups water

    3 tablespoons (30 gr) oatmeal

    1 tablespoon sunflower oil

    5 tablespoons + 2 teaspoons (80 gr) sugar

    1 teaspoon vanilla sugar or vanilla extract

    Pinch of sea salt

Preparation

1. Put the ingredients in the blender and process until smooth.
2. Strain as instructed in the basic recipe (page 12).

Oat Drink with Carob

Ingredients
  6 cups water
  3 tablespoons (30 gr) oatmeal
  1 ½ tablespoon (20 gr) carob flour
  1 tablespoon sunflower oil
  8 ½ tablespoons (130 gr) sugar
  1 teaspoon vanilla sugar or vanilla extract
  Pinch of sea salt

Preparation
1. Put the ingredients in the blender and process until smooth.
2. Strain as instructed in the basic recipe (page 12).

Oat Drink with Almonds

Ingredients
- 6 cups water
- 3 tablespoons (30 gr) oatmeal
- 6 tablespoons (50 gr) almonds
- 1 tablespoon sunflower oil
- 6 tablespoons (90 gr) sugar
- 1 teaspoon vanilla sugar or vanilla extract
- Pinch of sea salt

Preparation
1. Put the ingredients in the blender and process until smooth.
2. Strain as instructed in the basic recipe (page 12).

Oat Drink with Cocoa

Ingredients

    6 cups water

    3 tablespoons (30 gr) oatmeal

    2 tablespoons (20 gr) cocoa powder

    1 tablespoon sesame oil

    9 tablespoons (130 gr) sugar

    1 teaspoon vanilla sugar or vanilla extract

    Pinch of sea salt

Preparation

1. Put the ingredients in the blender and process until smooth.
2. Strain as instructed in the basic recipe (page 12).

Oat Drink with Cinnamon

Ingredients
6 cups water
3 tablespoons (30 gr) oatmeal
½ teaspoon ground cinnamon
1 tablespoon sunflower oil
5 tablespoons + 2 teaspoons (80 gr) sugar
1 teaspoon vanilla sugar or vanilla extract
Pinch of sea salt

Preparation
1. Put the ingredients in the blender and process until smooth.
2. Strain as instructed in the basic recipe (page 12).

Oat Drink with Malted Cereals

Ingredients
    6 cups water
    3 tablespoons (30 gr) oatmeal
    2 tablespoons malted cereals
    1 tablespoon sunflower oil
    7 tablespoons (100 gr) sugar
    1 teaspoon vanilla sugar or vanilla extract
    Pinch of sea salt

Preparation
1. Put the ingredients in the blender and process until smooth.
2. Strain as instructed in the basic recipe (page 12).

Oat Drink with Dehydrated Tropical Fruits

Ingredients

6 cups water
3 tablespoons (30 gr) oatmeal
⅔ cup (60 gr) dehydrated tropical fruits (papaya, coconut, pineapple, etc.)
1 tablespoon sunflower oil
5 tablespoons + 2 teaspoons (80 gr) sugar
1 teaspoon vanilla sugar or vanilla extract
Pinch of sea salt

Preparation
1. Put the ingredients in the blender and process until smooth.
2. Strain as instructed in the basic recipe (page 12).

Oat Drink with Lemon

Ingredients
- 6 cups water
- 3 tablespoons (30 gr) oatmeal
- The peel of a lemon
- 1 tablespoon sunflower oil
- 7 tablespoons (100 gr) sugar
- 1 teaspoon vanilla sugar or vanilla extract
- Pinch of sea salt

Preparation
1. Put the ingredients in the blender and process until smooth.
2. Strain as instructed in the basic recipe (page 12).

Relaxing Oat Drink

Ingredients
6 cups water
3 tablespoons (30 gr) oatmeal
1 tablespoon sesame oil
5 tablespoons + 2 teaspoons (80 gr) sugar
1 teaspoon vanilla sugar or vanilla exrtact
Pinch of sea salt

The Infusion
1¼ cup (300 ml) water
1 teaspoon chamomile flowers
1 teaspoon green aniseed
1 teaspoon mint

Preparation
1. **For the infusion:** Boil the water and add the herbs. Let steep for five minutes before straining.
2. Put the ingredients and the infusion in the blender. Process until smooth.
3. Strain as instructed in the basic recipe (page 12).

Oat Drink with Rosemary

Ingredients
> 5 ⅓ cups (1300 ml) water
> 3 tablespoons (30 gr) oatmeal
> 1 tablespoon sunflower oil
> 5 tablespoons + 2 teaspoons (80 gr) sugar
> Pinch of sea salt

The Infusion
> 1 cup (200 ml) water
> 1 tablespoon rosemary

Preparation
1. **For the infusion:** Boil the water. Turn off the heat and add the rosemary, letting it steep for five minutes before straining.
2. Put the ingredients and the infusion in the blender. Process until smooth.
3. Strain as instructed in the basic recipe (page 12).

BARLEY DRINKS

Benefits of Barley Drinks

Barley is another one of those cereals which you can transform into a nourishing drink. Enjoy it when it's cold, and if you are willing to try several varieties, add lemon, chocolate, etc., because these ingredients go very well with barley.

Of all the vegetable drinks you can make at home, this is one of the richest in protein content and one of the lowest in fat content. Thanks to its pH level of 6.15 to 6.8, it is very alkalizing, which is beneficial for the overall well-being of your body. One of the benefits is that it helps the muscles recover after a training session at the gym by combating acidosis. Therefore, it helps to fight muscular pains as well as arthritis, like rheumatoid or gout.

Barley provides a substantial amount of essential amino acids and tryptophan, which produces serotonin, a fundamental neurotransmitter that regulates ssleep and mood. This is one of the vegetable drinks richest in vitamins. It has vitamin B1 (for good skin), vitamin B2 (or riboflavin, responsible for cellular oxygenation), and vitamin B6 (also known as "pyroxene," important for the formation of red blood cells). In addition, it's rich in carotenes, which produce vitamin A.

It also contains a wide array of minerals (sodium, iron, manganese, potassium, etc.), ideal for fighting spring asthenia, and anemia. It also has isoflavones, ideal for promoting the production of estrogens, which help to regulate hormonal equilibrium in women.

It is recommended that you soak barley for six hours, if it is in grain form, and four hours if in the form of flakes.

FAR MORE THAN "BARLEY WATER"

Barley water is one of the most popular drinks in English speaking countries, used to fight colds and the flu. It's rich in minerals and helps soothe sore throats.

To prepare it, use a handful of barley and four cups of water. Bring it to a boil over medium heat. As soon as it boils, change the water and boil again for thirty minutes until the barley is well cooked and the liquid has reduced to one third. Strain, and it's ready to drink.

Add some honey to sweeten, and if you want you may add a little fruit juice. It keeps well up to a day or two in the refrigerator.

Although this is a refreshing and delicious beverage, you may also enjoy all the health benefits of barley in the form of its vegetable drink.

Basic Barley Drink Recipe

Ingredients

    6 cups water
    2.5 tablespoons (30 gr) pearled barley
    1 tablespoon sunflower oil
    5 tablespoons + 2 teaspoons (80 gr) sugar
    1 teaspoon vanilla sugar or vanilla extract
    Pinch of sea salt

Preparation

1. Put the ingredients in the blender and process until smooth.
2. Strain as instructed in the basic recipe (page 12).

Barley Drink with Lime

Ingredients

    6 cups water
    3 tablespoons (30 gr) pearled barley
    The peel of two small limes
    1 tablespoon sesame oil
    7 tablespoons (100 gr) sugar
    1 teaspoon vanilla sugar or vanilla extract
    Pinch of sea salt

Preparation

1. Put the ingredients in the blender and process until smooth.
2. Strain as instructed in the basic recipe (page 12).

Barley Drink with Coffee

Ingredients

    6 cups water
    3 tablespoons (30 gr) pearled barley
    1 tablespoon instant coffee
    1 tablespoon sunflower oil
    8 tablespoons (120 gr) sugar
    1 teaspoon vanilla sugar or vanilla extract
    Pinch of sea salt

Preparation

1. Put the ingredients in the blender and process until smooth.
2. Strain as instructed in the basic recipe (page 12).

Tips

- You can use decaffeinated coffee in this recipe, if you prefer. Or you may add more coffee to suit your taste; however, don't use more than two and a half tablespoons.
- You can also use one of several coffee substitutes (pages 115–118), among them malted drinks (pages 119–120).

Chicory is a good alternative to coffee.

Barley Drink with Coconut

Ingredients

    6 cups water
    3 tablespoons (30 gr) pearled barley
    ½ cup (50 gr) grated coconut
    1 tablespoon sunflower oil
    5 tablespoons + 2 teaspoons (80 gr) sugar
    1 teaspoon vanilla sugar or vanilla extract
    Pinch of sea salt

Preparation

1. Put the ingredients in the blender and process until smooth.
2. Strain as instructed in the basic recipe (page 12).

"Sweet Dreams" Barley Drink

Ingredients

    5 cups (1200 ml) water
    3 tablespoons (30 gr) pearled barley
    1 tablespoon sunflower oil
    5 tablespoons + 2 teaspoons (80 gr) sugar
    1 teaspoon vanilla sugar or vanilla extract
    Pinch of sea salt

The infusion

    1¼ cup (300 ml) water
    1 teaspoon linden flower tea
    1 teaspoon lemon balm
    1 teaspoon orange flowers
    1 teaspoon lemongrass

Preparation

1. **For the infusion:** Boil the water and add the herbs. Let steep for five minutes before straining.
2. Put the ingredients and the infusion in the blender. Process until smooth.
3. Strain as instructed in the basic recipe (page 12).

Lemon balm has good relaxant qualities.

Barley Drink with Wheat Germ

Ingredients

6 cups water
3 tablespoons (30 gr) pearled barley
50 gr wheat germ
1 tablespoon sesame oil
5 tablespoons + 2 teaspoons (80 gr) sugar
1 teaspoon vanilla sugar or vanilla extract
Pinch of sea salt

Preparation

1. Put the ingredients in the blender, except for the wheat germ. Process until smooth.
2. Add the wheat germ and process again.
3. Strain as instructed in the basic recipe (page 12).

Sesame has excellent nutritional qualities.

Barley Drink with Nuts

Ingredients

   6 cups water
   3 tablespoons (30 gr) pearled barley
   ¼ cup (30 gr) nuts
   1 tablespoon sunflower oil
   5 tablespoons + 2 teaspoons (80 gr) sugar
   1 teaspoon vanilla sugar or vanilla extract
   Pinch of sea salt

Preparation

1. Put the ingredients, except the walnuts, in the blender. Process until smooth.
2. Add the walnuts and process again.
3. Strain as instructed in the basic recipe (page 12).

Vanilla is a seed pod that turns black and exudes a great aroma when dried.

Barley Drink with Grapefruit

Ingredients

    6 cups water
    3 tablespoons (30 gr) pearled barley
    The peel of half a grapefruit (any variety)
    1 tablespoon sunflower oil
    7 tablespoons (100 gr) sugar
    1 teaspoon vanilla sugar or vanilla extract
    Pinch of sea salt

Preparation

1. Put the ingredients in the blender and process until smooth.
2. Strain as instructed in the basic recipe (page 12).

SOY DRINKS

Benefits of Soy Drinks

This is one of the "stars" of vegetable drinks. Soy drinks are some of the better-known and most widely consumed plant-based drinks in the world because of their rich, nourishing properties.

The soybean is a legume containing high quantities of proteins. Approximately thirty-six percent of it is composed of protein, making it the richest source (vegetable or animal) in the world. Moreover, they are high-quality proteins.

Soy drinks are a fantastic source of vitamins as well, such as vitamin A (an antioxidant and essential for bone and eye health), and vitamin E (an antioxidant). Its fat content is low, ideal for people trying to keep their weight under control.

Lecithin is one of its components. These are phospholipids that regulate cholesterol, fundamental for the proper health of cell walls, which are in charge of regulating what elements pass through the cells. If the cell walls are healthy, you will be protected against cellular oxidation.

With soy drinks as the base, there are many other nourishing and palatable products that can be prepared. For instance, you can make tofu, which is delicious both breaded and fried.

The following recipes for soy drinks can be kept in the refrigerator for up to four days. And if you want the drinks to have a subtle flavor, you may use pre-peeled soybeans.

OKARA: PURE PROTEIN

There is no food richer in protein than soybeans. When you strain the soy drink, you will see that the residue is like a semi-solid paste. Japanese call this paste "okara" (which is also a town in Japan), and it is the soy by-product richest in protein. It is used in countless Japanese recipes and is pure protein. Use it to enrich purées, as well as facial masks, for baking, etc.

Basic Soy Drink Recipe

Ingredients

    6 cups water
    ½ cup (90 gr) soy beans (white or yellow)
    1 tablespoon sunflower oil
    4 tablespoons (60 gr) sugar

Preparation

1. Put the soaked soy beans in the blender. Add all the ingredients and process until smooth.
2. Strain as instructed in the basic recipe (page 12).

Soy Drink with Carob

Ingredients

    6 cups water
    ½ cup (90 gr) soy beans (white or yellow)
    2 tablespoons (30 gr) carob flour
    1 tablespoon sunflower oil
    8 tablespoons (120 gr) sugar

Preparation

1. Put the soaked soy beans in the blender. Add all the ingredients and process until smooth.
2. Strain as instructed in the basic recipe (page 12).

Soy Drink for Well-Being

Ingredients
   6 cups water
   ½ cup (90 gr) soy beans (white or yellow)
   1 tablespoon sunflower oil
   6 tablespoons (90 gr) sugar

The Infusion
   1 cup water
   1 teaspoon green tea
   1 teaspoon mallow
   1 teaspoon green aniseed
   1 teaspoon elderberry

Preparation
1. Put the soaked soy beans in the blender. Add all the ingredients and process until smooth.
2. For the infusion: Boil the water and add the herbs. Let steep for two minutes, strain, and discard the residue.
3. Add the infusion to the blender and process again.
4. Strain as instructed in the basic recipe (page 12).

Malva flowers (in this photo *Malva arborea*) are used for decoration, but they also act as a mild laxative and detoxifier.

Soy Drink with Cocoa

Ingredients

    6 cups water
    ½ cup (90 gr) soy beans (white or yellow)
    2 tablespoons (20 gr) dark cocoa powder
    1 tablespoon sunflower oil
    8 1/2 tablespoons (130 gr) sugar

Preparation

1. Put the soaked soy beans in the blender. Add all the ingredients and process until smooth.
2. Strain as instructed in the basic recipe (page 12).

Calcium-Rich Soy Drink

Ingredients
6 cups water
½ cup (90 gr) soy beans (white or yellow)
⅔ cup (100 gr) sesame seeds
1 tablespoon sunflower oil
4 tablespoons (60 gr) sugar

Preparation
1. Put the soaked soy beans in the blender. Add all the ingredients except the sesame seeds and process until smooth.
2. Add the sesame and process again.
3. Strain as instructed in the basic recipe (page 12).

Tip
You may add more sesame seeds for an extra calcium boost.

Did you know?
The calcium in sesame seeds is of high quality and is easily absorbed by the body because it's organic and natural. You can buy vegetable drinks that are enriched with calcium, but they are artificial; therefore, calcium absorption is minimal.

Sunflower oil: beneficial to your health.

Soy Drink for Cholesterol Control

Ingredients
6 cups water
½ cup (90 gr) soy beans (white or yellow)
5 ½ tablespoons (80 gr) soy lecithin
1 tablespoon sunflower oil
4 tablespoons (60 gr) sugar

Preparation
1. Put the soaked soy beans in the blender. Add all the ingredients and process until smooth.
2. Strain as instructed in the basic recipe (page 12).

Did you know?
Soy lecithin is fantastic for lowering high cholesterol levels. It also helps with the assimilation of fats and to get rid of them in an efficient manner.

Soy and its derivatives.

Soy Drink with Wild Fruits

Ingredients
- 6 cups water
- ½ cup (90 gr) soy beans (white or yellow)
- 1 cup (100 gr) wild fruits
- 1 tablespoon sunflower oil
- 8 tablespoons (100 gr) sugar

Preparation
1. Put the soaked soy beans in the blender. Add all the ingredients, except the fruits, and process until smooth.
2. Add the fruits and process again.
3. Strain as instructed in the basic recipe (page 12).

Wild fruits (like gooseberries, blueberries, raspberries, and wild strawberries) and red fruits (like strawberries, cherries, and plums) give soybean smoothies an appealing flavor.

Soy Drink with Dehydrated Fruits

Ingredients

6 cups water
½ cup (90 gr) soy beans (white or yellow)
1 ⅓ cup (120 gr) dehydrated fruits (papaya, pineapple, coconut, banana, etc.)
1 tablespoon sunflower oil
4 tablespoons (60 gr) sugar

Preparation

1. Put the soaked soy beans in the blender. Add all the ingredients and process until smooth.
2. Strain as instructed in the basic recipe (page 12).

Soy Drink with Dried Fruits

Ingredients

    6 cups water
    ½ cup (90 gr) soy beans (white or yellow)
    ¾ cup (100 gr) dried fruits (raisins, plum, peach, pear, etc.)
    1 tablespoon sunflower oil
    4 tablespoons (60 gr) sugar

Preparation

1. Put the soaked soy beans in the blender. Add all the ingredients and process until smooth.
2. Strain as instructed in the basic recipe (page 12).

Soy Drink with Fresh Pineapple

Ingredients

    6 cups water
    ½ cup (90 gr) soy beans (white or yellow)
    1 cup (120 gr) fresh pineapple, chopped
    1 tablespoon sunflower oil
    6 tablespoons (90 gr) sugar

Preparation

1. Put the soaked soy beans in the blender. Add all the ingredients and process until smooth.
2. Strain as instructed in the basic recipe (page 12)

Soy Drink with Nuts

Ingredients

    6 cups water
    ½ cup (90 gr) soy beans (white or yellow)
    ⅔ cup (80 gr) nuts (almonds, hazelnuts, walnuts, etc.)
    1 tablespoon sunflower oil
    4 tablespoons (60 gr) sugar

Preparation

1. Put the soaked soy beans in the blender. Add all the ingredients, except the nuts, and process until smooth.
2. Add the nuts and process again.
3. Strain as instructed in the basic recipe (page 12).

Soy Drink with Lemon

Ingredients

    6 cups water
    ½ cup (90 gr) soy beans (white or yellow)
    The peel of a lemon
    1 tablespoon sunflower oil
    4 tablespoons (60 gr) sugar

Preparation

1. Put the soaked soy beans in the blender. Add all the ingredients and process until smooth.
2. Strain as instructed in the basic recipe (page 12).

Soy Drink with Orange

Ingredients

    6 cups water
    ½ cup (90 gr) soy beans (white or yellow)
    The peel of an orange
    1 tablespoon sunflower oil
    4 tablespoons (60 gr) sugar

Preparation

1. Put the soaked soy beans in the blender. Add all the ingredients and process until smooth.
2. Strain as instructed in the basic recipe (page 12).

Soy Drink with Green Tea and Mint

Ingredients

6 cups water
½ cup (90 gr) soy beans (white or yellow variety)
3 dried mint leaves
1 tablespoon sunflower oil
6 tablespoons (90 gr) sugar

The Tea

1 cup water
1 teaspoon green tea

Preparation

1. **First brew the tea:** Bring the water to a boil, turn off the heat, and steep for two minutes. Let cool.
2. Put the soaked soy beans in the blender. Add all the ingredients and process until smooth.
3. Strain as instructed in the basic recipe (page 12).

OTHER VEGETABLE DRINKS

Spring of Health

It is very easy to make several vegetable drink varieties at home. The only appliance you need is a blender or a food processor in order to process all the ingredients. The following recipes are even easier than the previous ones, so you can learn to make and enjoy different drinks.

Chufa Nut Horchata

The classic and refreshing chufa nut horchata is also a healthy vegetable drink. It originated in Valencia, Spain, and from there it was exported to the world. Today, the US and France are among its largest consumers.

The secret behind this delicious beverage is in the actual chufa (*Cyperus esculentus*), a tuber of the cyperaceous family. It is so highly valued in Valencia that there exists the Regulatory Council of the Denomination of Origin Valencia Chufa, which controls its production. This chufa horchata must be made with chufa harvested in one of sixteen Valencian towns, in the shire of Horta Nord.

Horchata is a great beverage for the hot days of summer, and it's also very revitalizing thanks to its high carbohydrate content. It has unsaturated fats and oleic acids, which assist in controlling cholesterol and triglyceride levels in the blood. Its consumption is highly recommended during times of high mental activity because it is rich in phosphorus and potassium, which nourish the brain.

But where does that name come from? Tradition says that a young lady gave this delicious beverage to King Jaume I. Upon tasting it, the monarch exclaimed, in Catalan: "Això és or, xata," which in Spanish translates as "Esto es oro, chata." (This is gold, little one.)

Ingredients

  6 cups water
  325 gr chufa
  ¾ cup (175 gr) sugar
  4 cups water (to soak chufa)

Preparation

1. Place the chufas and 4 cups water in a bowl for twenty-four hours. This will get rid of any remaining soil.
2. Drain the chufas and put in the blender. Process the remaining water and sugar.
3. Strain as instructed in the basic recipe (page 12).
4. Process any remaining solids and strain again.
5. Repeat once more, transfer to a jar and keep refrigerated.
6. Serve the horchata cold. Shake or stir before serving because it tends to settle in the bottom of the jar.

Tip

To add a little zing to your horchata, add a pinch of ground cinnamon or lemon zest to the mixture.

Almond Drink

Without a doubt, almond drinks are some of the tastiest and healthiest you can make. Among its many virtues, it fortifies bones thanks to its high calcium and phosphorus content, which makes it highly recommended for people suffering from osteoporosis. Children and teenagers will benefit as well. Serve this drink with cereal or muesli at breakfast or as a snack. If they are persistent, add a small amount of sweetener, like sugar or honey, to make it more palatable for them.

Additionally, it's ideal for pregnant women and for those who are breastfeeding, because it promotes lactation. It is easily digested and good for people who are ill or for those recovering from an illness.

On the other hand, almond drinks are rich in "good fats" (about twenty percent of its fats are polyunsaturated), which are highly recommended for keeping cholesterol under control. It is a vegetable drink that can be enjoyed any time of the day, but its high protein content, and its invigorating potential, make it ideal to have early in the morning.

Ingredients
    6 cups water
    2 ½ cups (200 gr) almonds
    7 tablespoons (100 gr) sugar
    1 tablespoon (30 gr) vanilla sugar or vanilla extract

Preparation
1. Peel the almonds and make sure they are dry before processing them. Process until finely ground.
2. Add ⅓ of the water, sugar, and vanilla sugar/extract, and process until smooth.

3. Strain as instructed in the basic recipe (page 12).
4. Add the remaining water and process again with all the solids.
5. Repeat the previous step. Transfer the liquid to a jar and keep refrigerated.

Hazelnut Drink

Hazelnuts are one of the most popular nuts. They are not only flavorful but also very healthy. They are harvested in the fall, and they need to be dried for a year before consumption.

Like any other nut, they are great for people with kidney issues. They are rich in magnesium that helps eliminate kidney stones. In addition to that, they are rich in one of the strongest antioxidants, vitamin E, which helps fight aging and makes the skin look young and vibrant.

It's wise to increase one's consumption of hazelnuts to regulate cholesterol and triglyceride levels because they are rich in polyunsaturated fats. Furthermore, they are recommended for both children and adults for their calcium content. For digestive problems, it is sensible to enrich the diet with hazelnuts because their folic acid and fiber aid in digestion.

It is best to buy hazelnuts whole and store them in tightly sealed tins, in the dark. This method will preserve them longer.

Ingredients
>   4 cups water
>   1 ¾ cup (200 gr) hazelnuts
>   Juice of 1 lemon
>   7 tablespoons (100 gr) sugar
>   2 cups water (to soak the hazelnuts)

Preparation
1. Peel the hazelnuts. Put them in a bowl with 2 cups water and soak for at least two hours.

2. Drain and process with the remaining water.
3. Strain as instructed in the basic recipe (page 12).
4. Add sugar and lemon juice, then stir until smooth.
5. Put in a jar and keep in the refrigerator.

Tip
Sometimes, peeling hazelnuts is rather difficult. To make this an easier task, boil the nuts for five minutes, and when they cool to lukewarm, the skin will be very easy to peel.

Coconut Drink

A delicious fruit from the tropics, coconut makes a nutrient rich and delicious drink, and it's incredibly easy to prepare. Coconut drinks are good for bone and teeth problems. Moreover, they are extraordinary for children and teenagers. A glass a day is excellent for bones and overall health, and very soon you will notice the difference.

They are rich in polyunsaturated fats that help to reduce cholesterol levels in the blood. Your skin will glow with a healthful and youthful look.

If you are a sport aficionado or lead a busy life, coconut drinks will boost your energy levels. Drink a glass before heading to the gym, or afterwards to rejuvenate your muscles.

Coconut drinks can be consumed on their own or as part of a smoothy. Add ⅓ coconut juice to your smoothies. This will boost the nutritional powers of any smoothie, and will give it a delicious, tropical flavor.

Ingredients

- 6 cups boiling water
- 1 ½ cup (250 gr) fresh coconut
- 5 tablespoons + 2 teaspoons (80 gr) sugar
- 1 tablespoon vanilla sugar or vanilla extract

Preparation

1. Grate the coconut or process in a blender.
2. Transfer to a saucepan of boiling water and boil for fifteen minutes. Turn off the heat and let rest for twenty minutes.
3. Strain as instructed in the basic recipe (page 12).
4. Process the liquid and the solids again, and strain one more time.
5. Repeat the previous step. Transfer the liquid to a jar and keep refrigerated.

Tip

To extract the coconut flesh, cut the coconut in half and heat it on the stove. This is the easiest way to extract the flesh.

Corn Drink

Corn is one of the most extensively grown crops in the world, and it is a dietary staple of many cultures, especially in Latin American countries. There are several species, but all of them come from *Zea diploperennia*, native to central Mexico.

The historical importance of corn is such that five-thousand-year-old corn vases have been uncovered at archeological sites. It is believed that the word *maíz* comes from Taíno, whose roots are in Haiti, meaning "the one who sustains life."

Corn is rich in starch and carbohydrates. It is filling and recommended in weight loss diets because it keeps you feeling fuller for longer. Its fiber content helps to fight constipation. Thanks to its high vitamin B content, it is also good for the skin.

Ingredients
4 cups water
¾ cup (100 gr) fresh corn
Juice of 1 lemon
2 tablespoons honey

Preparation
1. Bring the water to a boil over medium heat. Add the corn and cook for fifteen minutes. Transfer to a blender and process until smooth.
2. Strain as instructed in the basic recipe (page 12). Cool.
3. Add lemon juice and honey, stir and keep refrigerated.

Did you know?

Corn is the base of many beverages; one of the oldest is called *atole*, a pre-Hispanic drink popular in Mexico and Central America. It is made with ground corn, water, and sugar and cooked until it is thick. It is traditionally served hot.

Millet tart. Millet is a nutrient-rich cereal and is enjoyable as a beverage.

Millet Drink

Millet is one of the oldest cereals known to man. It became the first crop native to Central Africa because of its ability to withstand droughts. In addition, it has a long shelf life and doesn't lose its nutritious properties.

Millet is widely harvested in India and China where it was introduced by Arab merchants in the Middle Ages. It is believed that millet feeds more than four hundred million people, and it is often used to substitute rice.

It's rich in proteins (it has more than rice but less than wheat). Furthermore, millet has minerals such as phosphorus, iron, and magnesium; at the same time, it's rich in vitamins A and B, and has a high content of eight essential amino acids. These nutrients make it a great aid in strengthening bones, hair, and eyesight.

On the other hand, millet is very easy to digest because it's highly alkaline. And since it is nutrient dense, it is a wonderful food for pregnant women.

If you want to include this wonderful cereal in your diet, make rice and millet soups. It mixes nicely with other vegetables.

Ingredients

- 4 cups water
- 1 ½ cup (300 gr) millet
- 2 cups (300 gr) sprouted sunflower seeds
- 1 tablespoons honey
- Pinch of ground spirulina

Preparation

1. Put the millet, sunflower, spirulina, and water in the blender. Process until smooth.
2. Strain as instructed in the basic recipe (page 12). Let cool.
3. Add honey, stir, and keep refrigerated.

Did you know?

Spirulina (*Spirulina maxima*) is a seaweed that grows naturally in alkaline environments and is packed with nutrients, like B vitamins, iron, magnesium, and zinc. It comes from Hawaii and from Mexican lakes but is also harvested in many other countries. Its name refers to its spiral form—it has a green-blue color thanks to chlorophyll and other compounds. You can find it in powder form or in pills.

Spirulina harvest in Niger.

TEA AND COFFEE SUBSTITUTES

Tea and coffee are the most consumed beverage in the world. From Japan to Canada and from Iceland to South Africa, every day millions of people drink cups and cups of coffee and tea.

We consume these drinks not only for their stimulant properties, but also because we have associated them with moments of rest, escape, and pleasure. Both are stimulating drinks, so they should not be abused. It's not that you should stop consuming them, but you should practice moderation.

Maybe you love to drink a good morning coffee, or a cup of tea or coffee with milk after breakfast. These are your routines, your small pleasures, and it's understandable that you are not willing to give them up. And you don't have to. You can still get the same pleasure by opting (even if only occasionally) for vegetable drinks.

Nutritionists claim that it is advisable to avoid coffee whenever possible. In any case, it is advisable not to abuse this drink, as numerous studies have demonstrated that it is harmful to the nervous system and stomach, for example, and facilitates calcium loss.

Traditionally, three herbs have been used to replace coffee: chicory, cleavers, and acorns. Remember that drinks you get with these herbs will have a very bitter taste, so sweetening them will surely be necessary.

Chicory is a good coffee substitute, and it's great as a cleanser.

Toasted and crushed chicory roots have been used to give a different flavor to coffee since the eighteenth century. Moreover, in times when there has been a shortage of coffee, chicory has been used as a substitute. To prepare an infusion of chicory, you have to let the roots dry. Then, clean them and toast them in a preheated oven, at medium heat. Let them cool when they are toasted and then grind them into a fine powder. Finally, mix one cup of boiling water per teaspoon of ground chicory, and strain.

Acorns: a natural coffee substitute.

Another option is cleavers. The seeds of this plant are an excellent substitute for coffee and belong to the same family as Rubiaceae. Toast the seeds of cleavers in the oven at moderate temperature and then let cool. Then grind them and mix a cup of boiling water per teaspoon of ground cleavers. Finally, strain it.

You can also prepare an alternative to coffee with acorns. Get them fresh and toast them in moderate heat. Once cold, grind them and add a teaspoon of crushed acorns per cup of boiling water. Strain before serving.

Green tea is rich in antioxidants and low in theophylline (equivalent to the caffeine of coffee), making it both soothing and stimulating. As alternatives to tea—particularly black tea—you have, for example, a number of plants that do not contain tea's stimulant properties, and instead are as healthy as they are delicious.

To prepare some herbal teas, you can decoct it by placing the herbs in boiling water. Let it stand for a few minutes before straining. You can prepare infusions of mint, marjoram, rosemary, nettle, sage, elderberry, etc. It is simply a matter of determining which infusions you prefer and combining them to create new flavors and aromas.

Hierbabuena—a type of mint—is not only tasty but very good on its own or combined with green tea.

How to Make Malt Drinks

Undoubtedly, malted drinks are the most popular and widespread alternatives to coffee, and for this reason we have devoted a special section to it. Although you can prepare many cereal malts, it is customary to use barley because it contains the most starches that transform into sugars.

Also, keep in mind an important distinction when buying packaged malt. "Malt," in this case, is the germinated product with which malt drinks are made. The malt drink is what you will substitute your coffee with.

Barley is the only cereal which is not used to prepare bread since the protein it contains does not have gluten. Without gluten, the gas produced by fermenting yeast is not retained and the dough fails to rise.

You can prepare malt drinks at home in a very simple way:

1. First, let the barley soak in warm water for twelve hours, at a minimum.
2. Then, leave it in a moist bag or porous cloth.
3. Now, leave the barley on the counter or a saucer or dish large enough so that it is not too piled up. The barley's temperature should be kept between 62°F and 68°F for ten days. In addition, you should spray it with warm water from time to time, without soaking it entirely. If the temperature exceeds 62°F, the barley will expand and form a wider layer. If the temperature falls below 68°F, pile it up a bit.
4. After ten days, the barley will doubled in size. Then, bake the barley at low temperature and with the door open to allow for airflow and to let it dry more easily.
5. When the barley is dry, bake it at moderate heat or toast it in a pan.
6. Now you only have to grind it in order to have a suitable malt with which to combine your choice of infusion. You can add, for example, one teaspoon of malt per cup of water.

Malt beverages have a slightly bitter taste that may not be enjoyed by everyone. To sweeten it, it is advisable to opt for a little honey. It is best not to add sugar so you can enjoy the diuretic and tonic properties of this healthy drink.

Malt's or "barley coffee's" characteristic bubbles.

NOTES